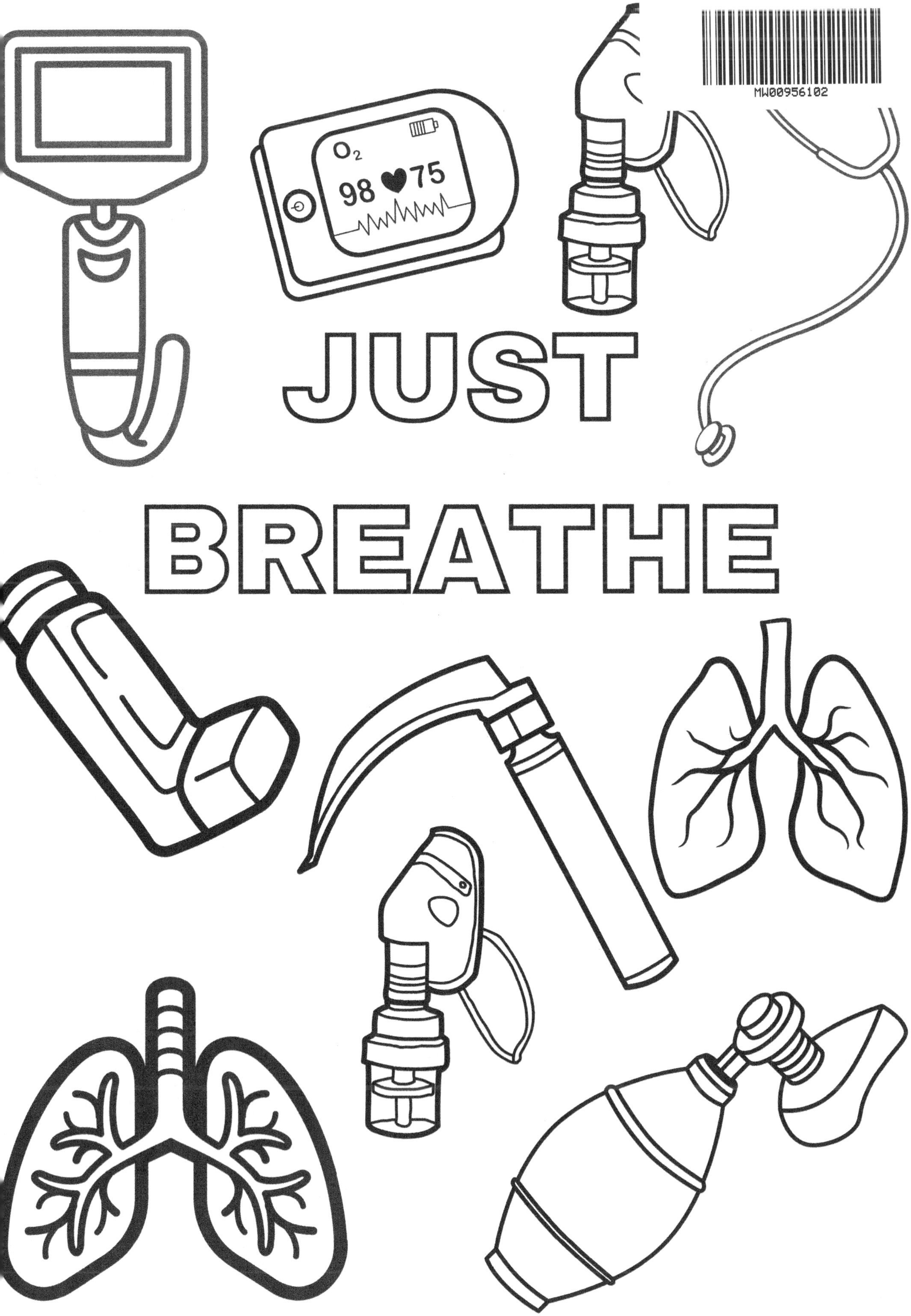
JUST
BREATHE
O2
98 75

NEBULIZER

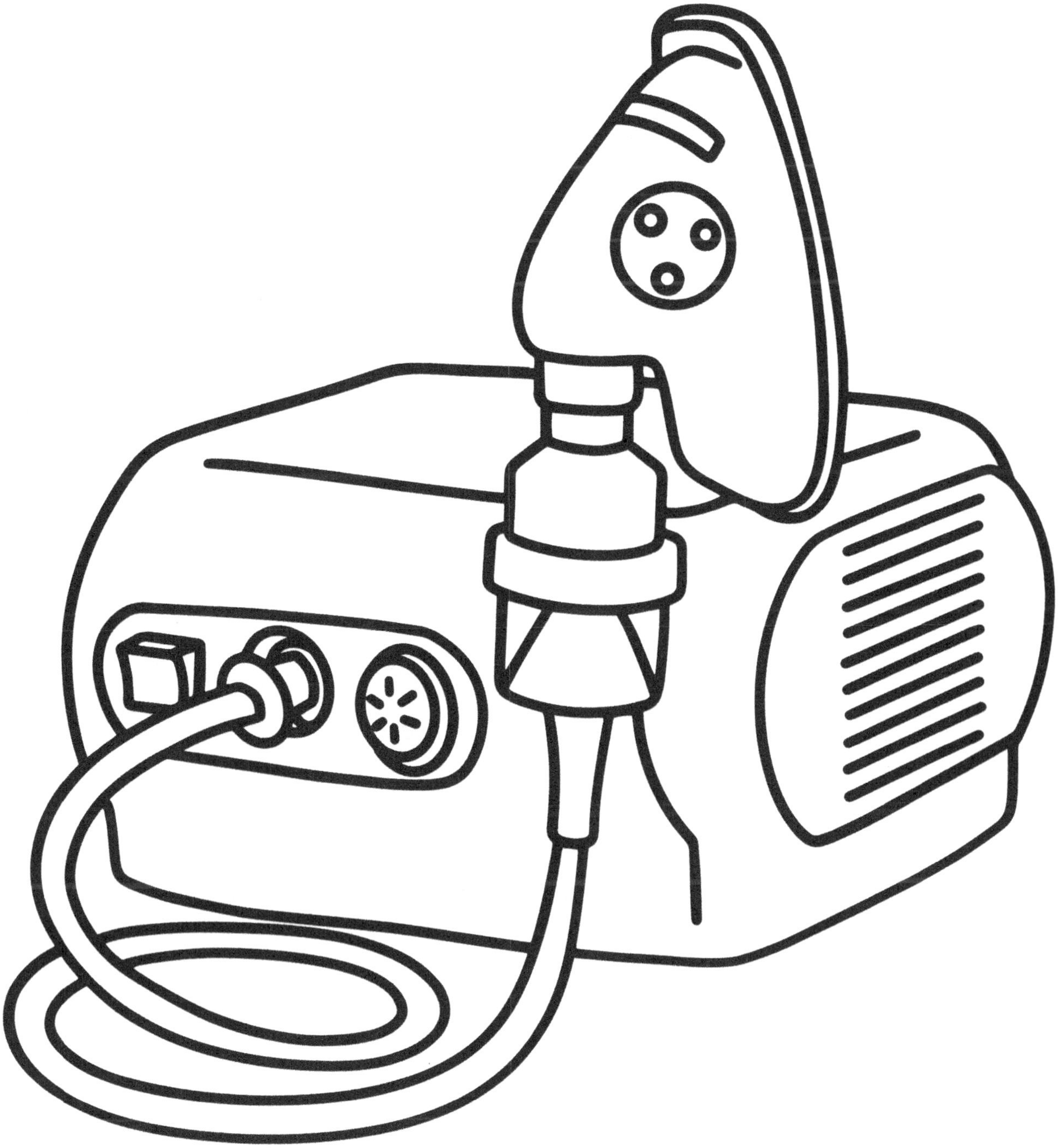

OXYGEN DEVICES

VENTILATOR

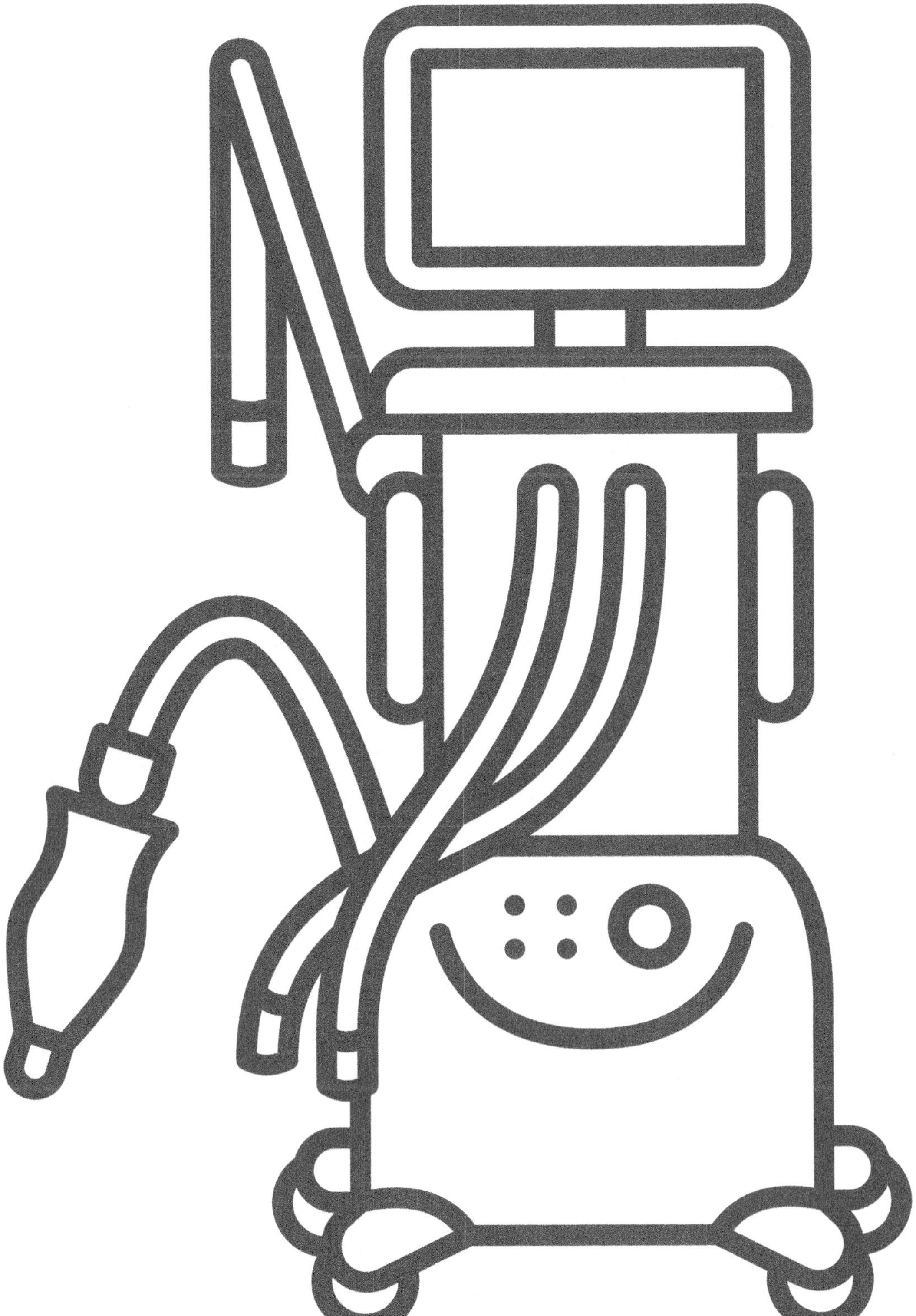

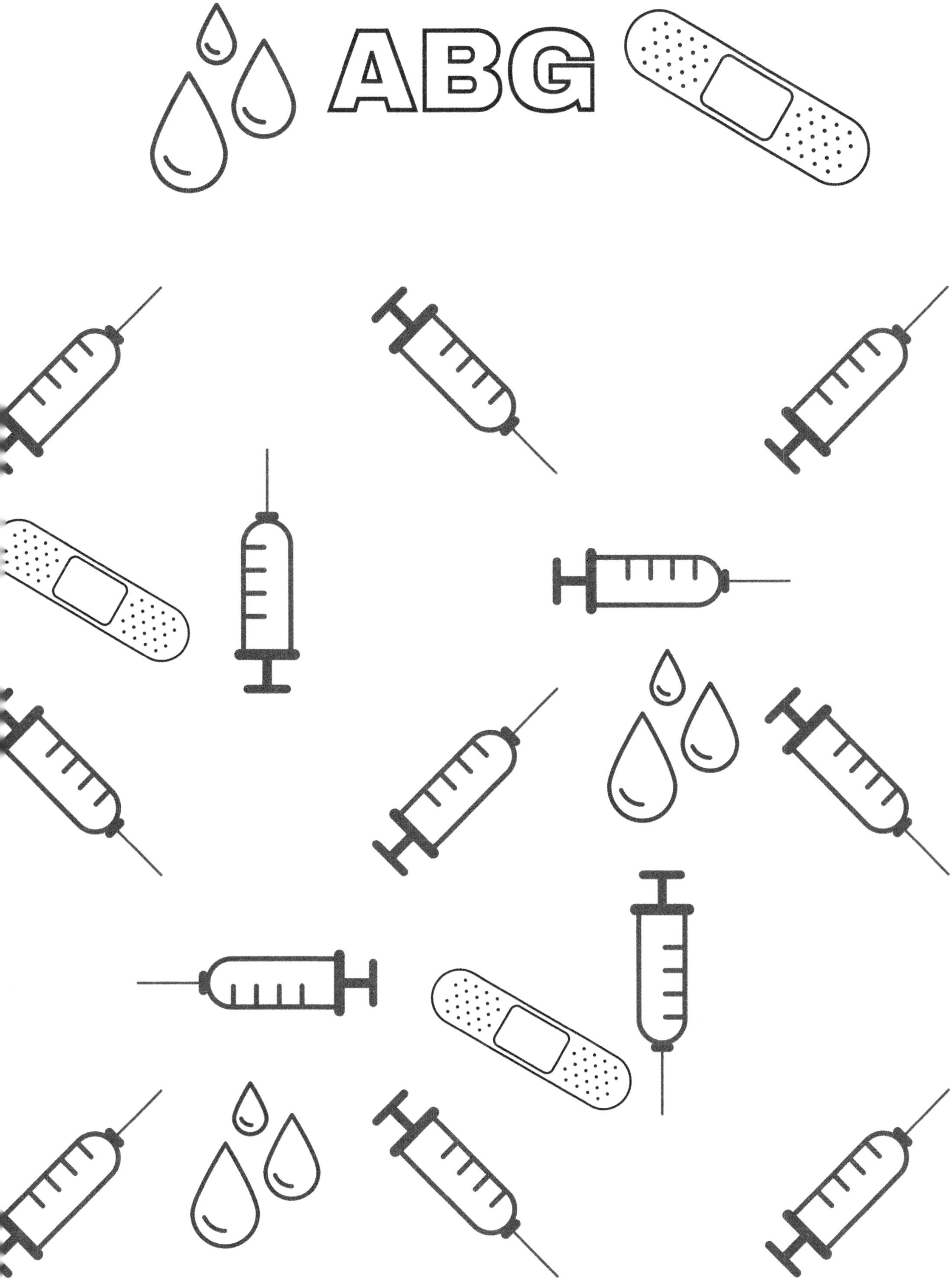
ABG

CHEST X-RAY

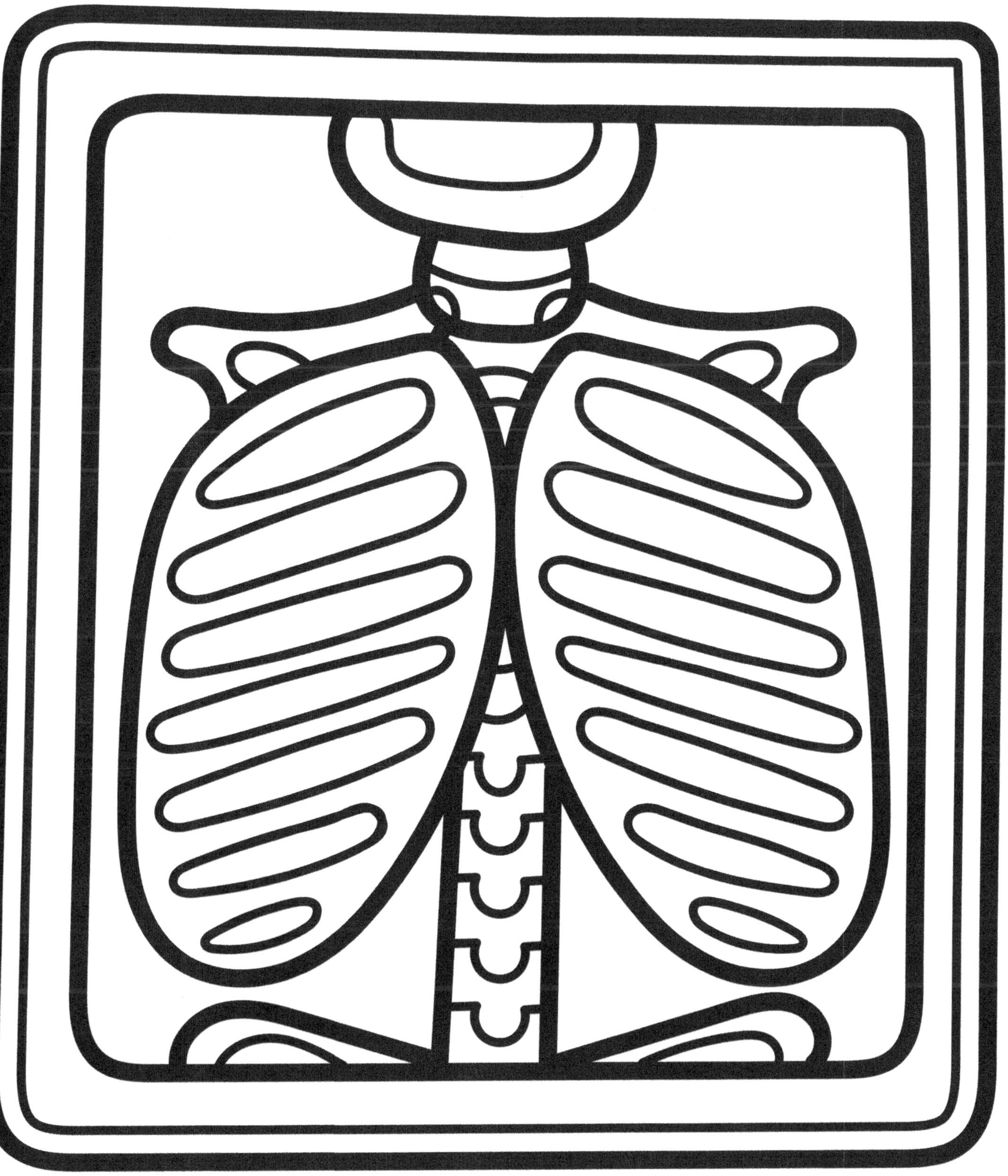

INHALER

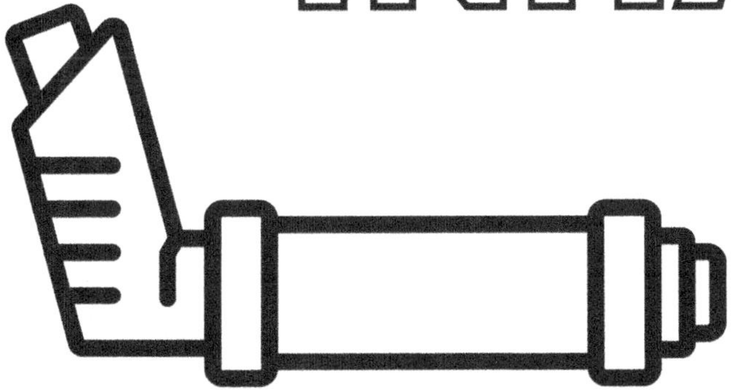

SCRUBS

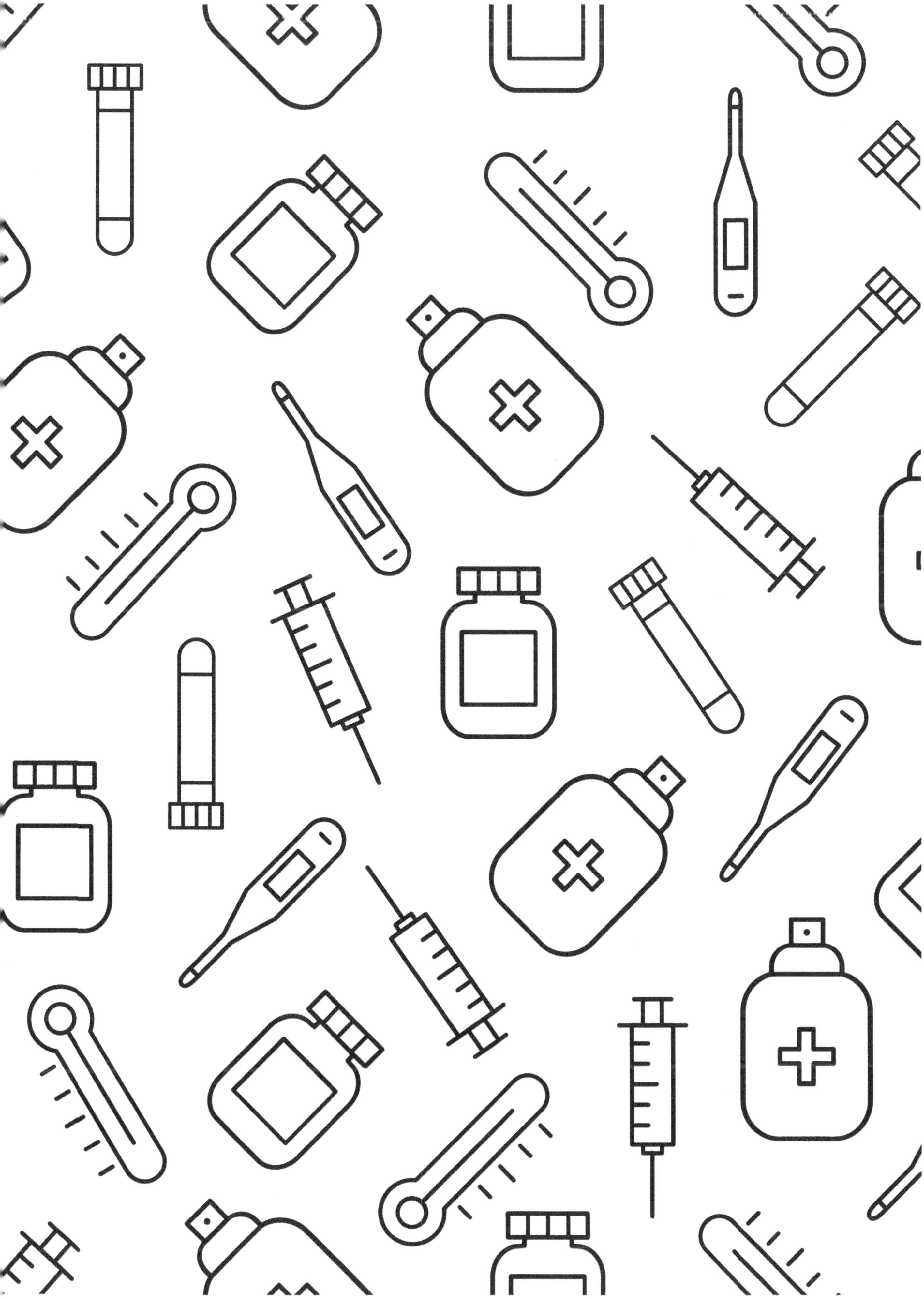

PPE

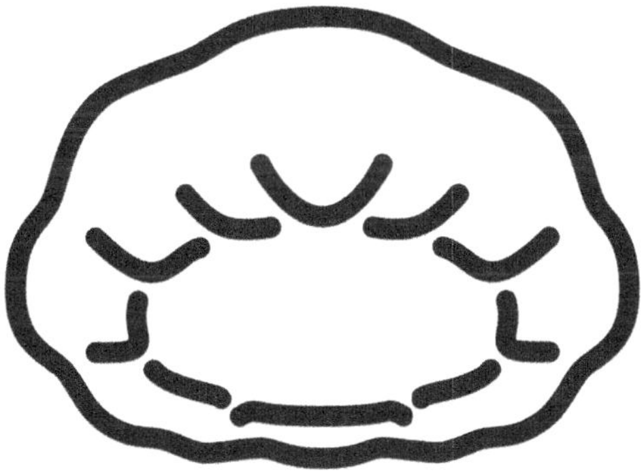

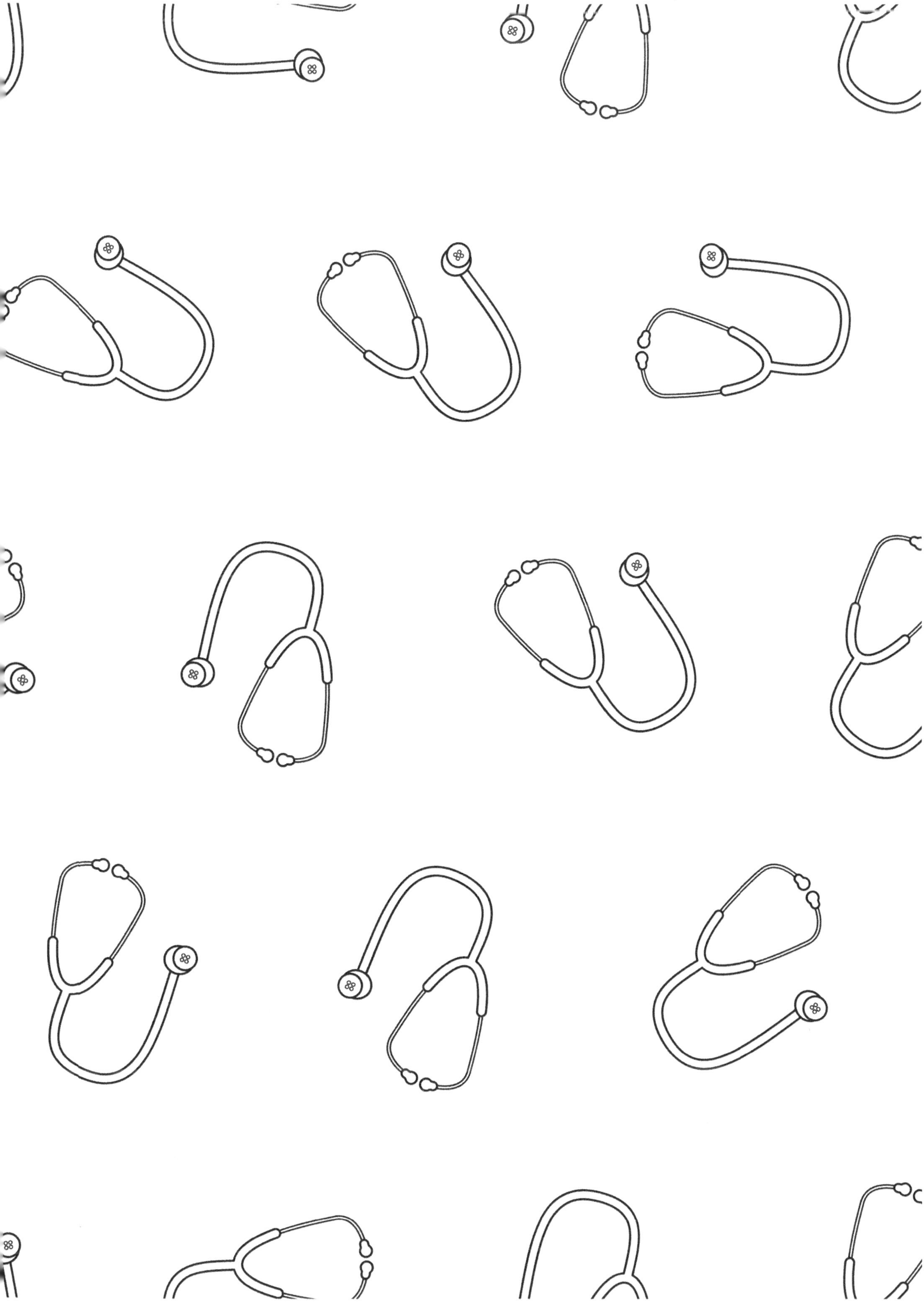

CPR

CPAP
ZZZ..)

LUNGS

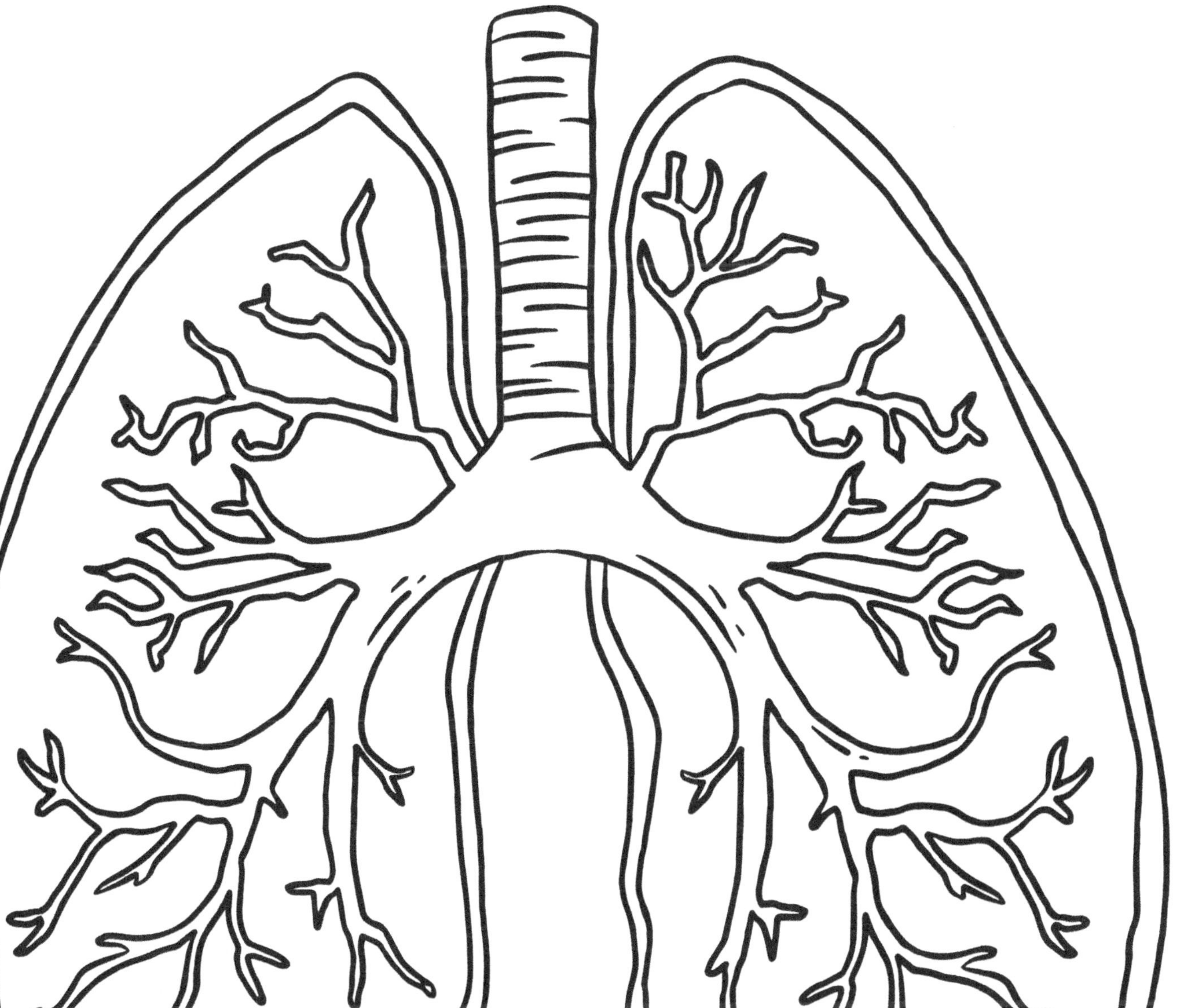

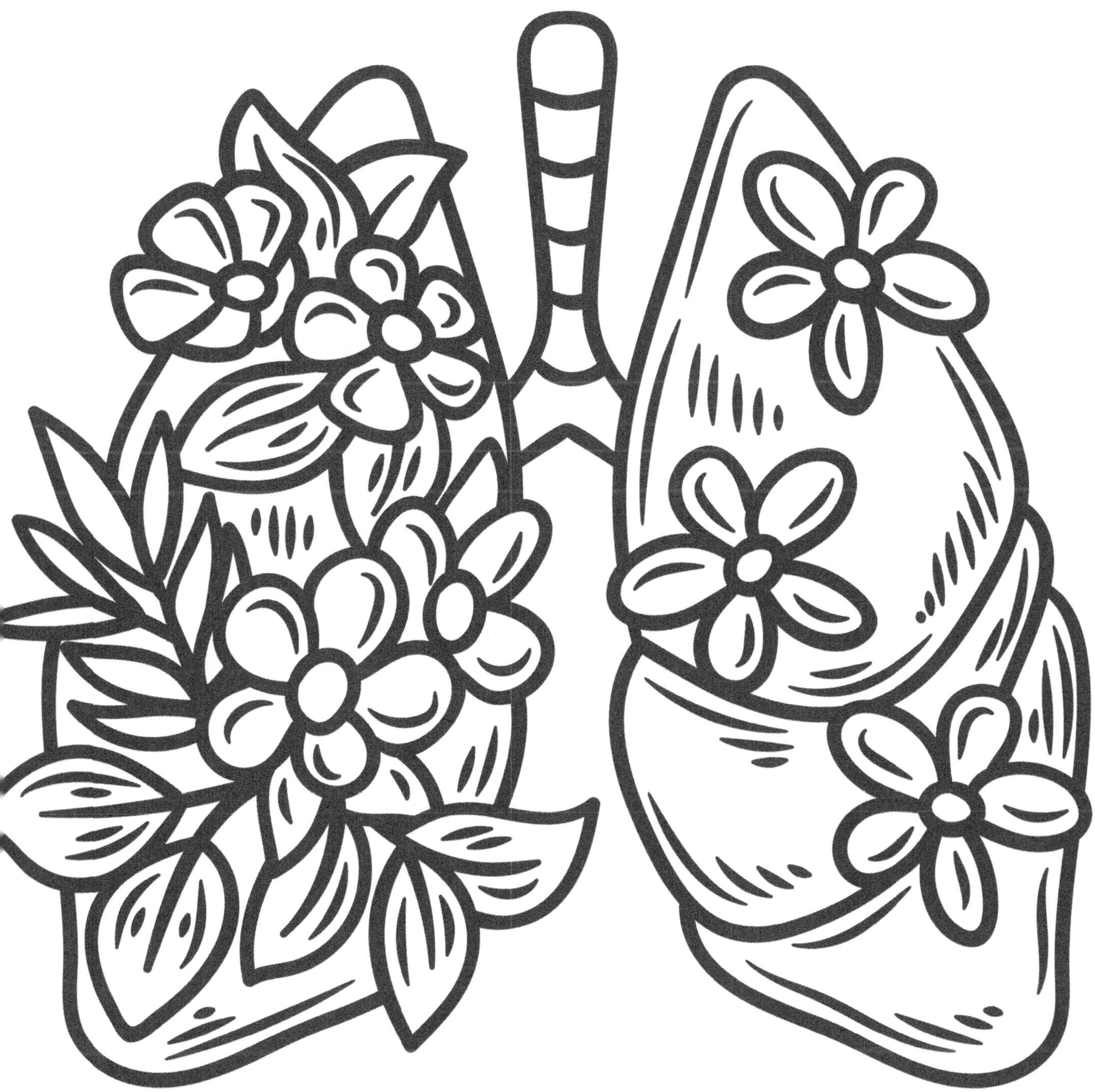

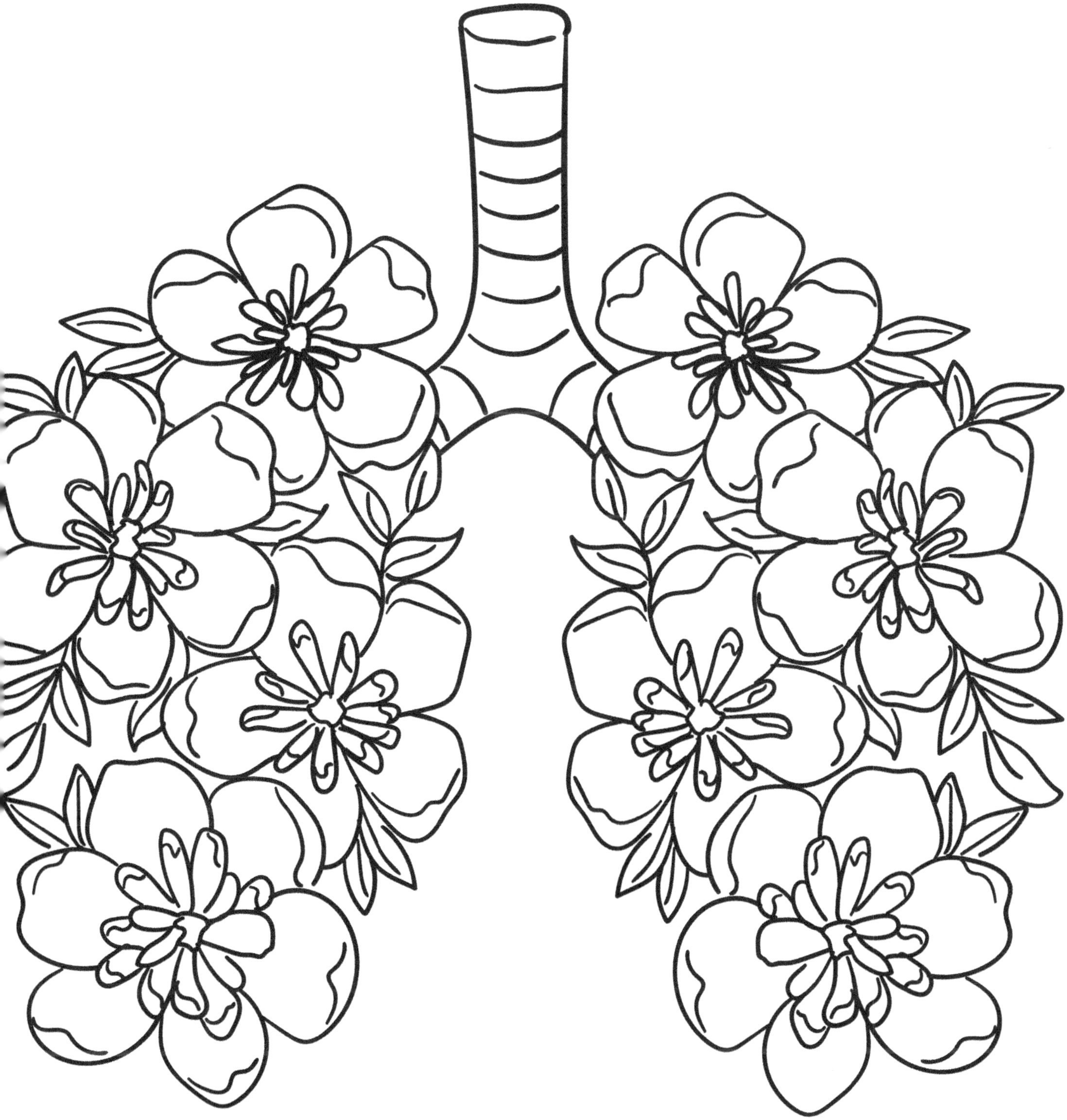

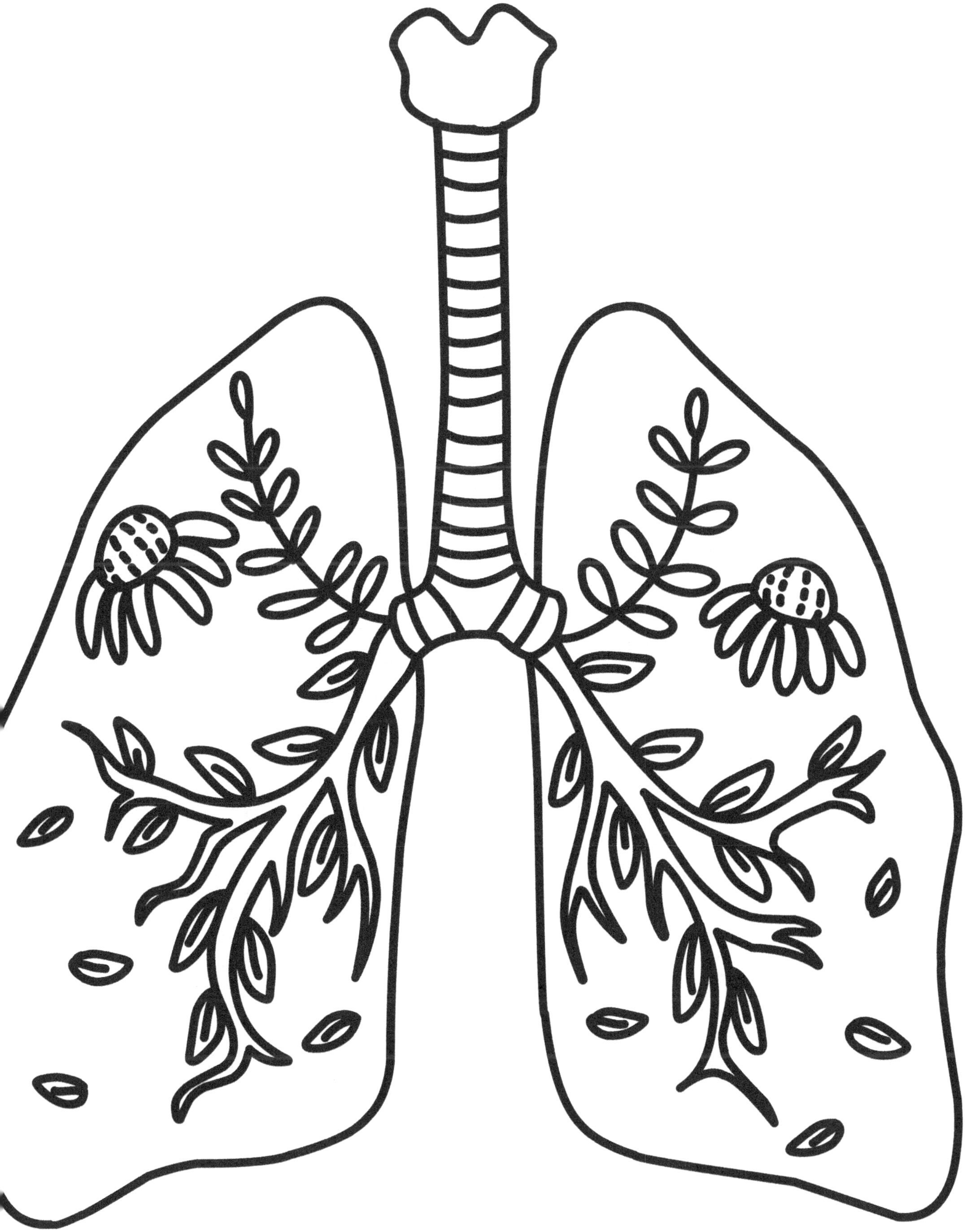

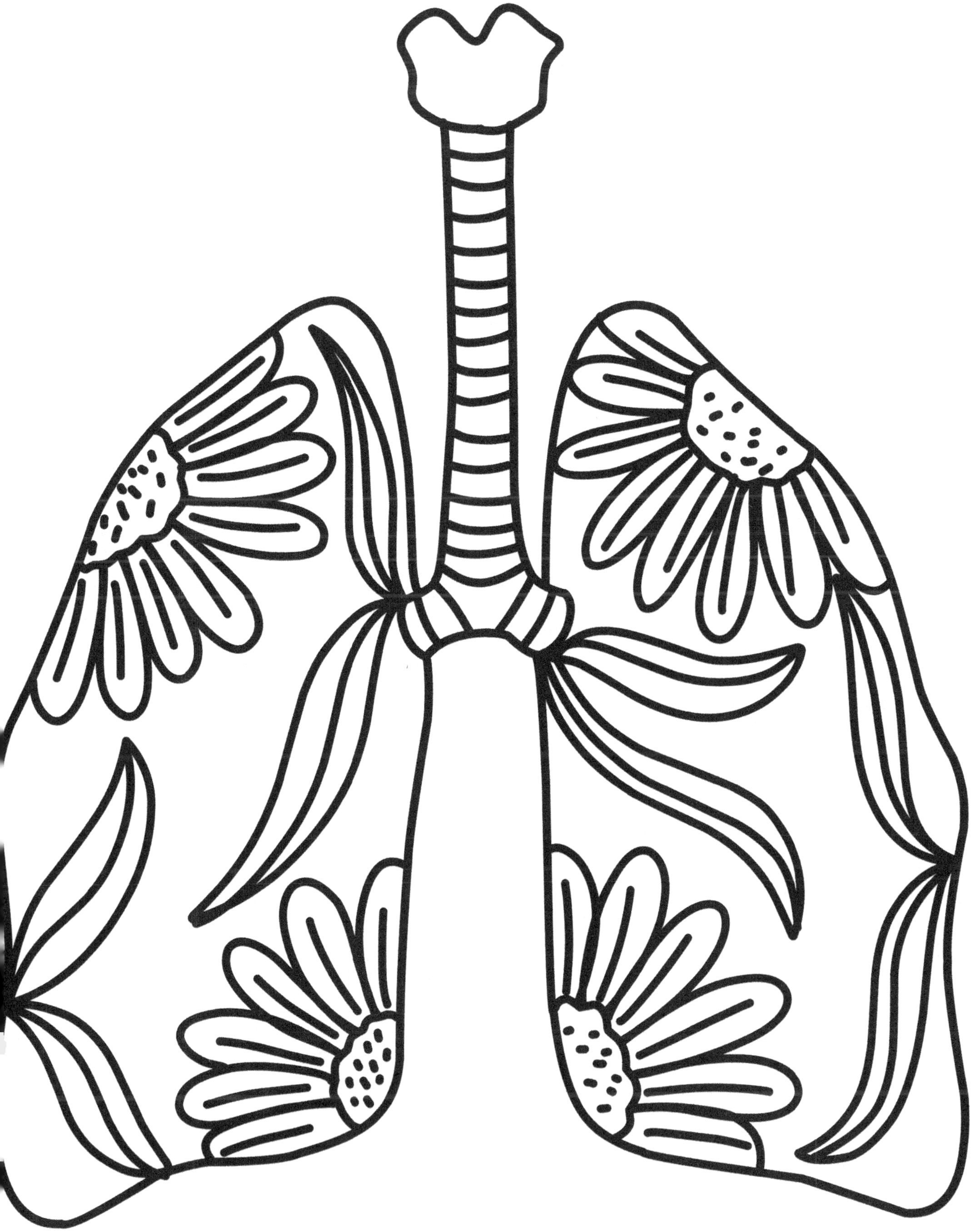

Made in the USA
Monee, IL
02 August 2024

63157568R00031